A New True Book

ENDANGERED ANIMALS

By Lynn M. Stone

CHILDREN'S PRESS
A Division of Grolier Publishing
Sherman Turnpike
Danbury, Connecticut 06816

Loggerhead turtle

FOR MUFF

Acknowledgment:
The author wishes to acknowledge the help of the Brookfield Zoo and the Brookfield Children's Zoo, Brookfield, Illinois, in the preparation of this book.

PHOTO CREDITS

Lynn M. Stone—2, 4 (2 photos), 8 (2 photos), 9 (2 photos), 10 (right), 16, 18 (2 photos), 19 (right), 21 (right), 23 (right), 24 (2 photos), 25 (2 photos), 26 (bottom right), 29 (2 photos), 33 (2 photos), 35 (2 photos), 37, 38 (right), 39 (2 photos), 40 (top), 41, 43, 44 (bottom left)

© 1979 Blue Whale Expedition, Marine Mammal Fund—31

James Rowan—Cover, 12 (right), 19 (left), 20 (2 photos), 21 (left), 23 (left), 38 (left), 40 (bottom), 44 (top)

Historical Pictures Service, Chicago—6 (2 photos)

Nawrocki Stock Photo—© 1983 Jeffrey Apoian, 10 (left), 14, 26 (bottom left)

Reinhard Brucker—26 (top)

Joseph A. DiChello, Jr.—12 (left)

Hillstrom Stock Photos—© 1983 Ray Hillstrom, 17, 44 (bottom right)

Cover—White Rhino

Library of Congress Cataloging in Publication Data

Stone, Lynn M.
    Endangered animals.

    (A New true book)
    Includes index.
    Summary: Discusses various endangered animal species in the world, why and how they became endangered, and what can be done to save them.
    1. Endangered species—Juvenile literature.
2. Rare animals—Juvenile literature. [1. Rare animals.
2. Wildlife conservation] I. Title.
QL83.S76 1984   333.95'4   83-26323
ISBN 0-516-01724-1   AACR2

TABLE OF CONTENTS

Siberian tiger

Bengal tiger swimming

ANIMALS IN DANGER

Tigers are in trouble. In Asia, where they live in the wild, tigers are disappearing. Someday there may not be any wild tigers at all.

The tiger is not the only animal in trouble. There are hundreds of other animals that are endangered. Endangered means they are in danger of becoming extinct. If all the animals of a kind die, that kind of

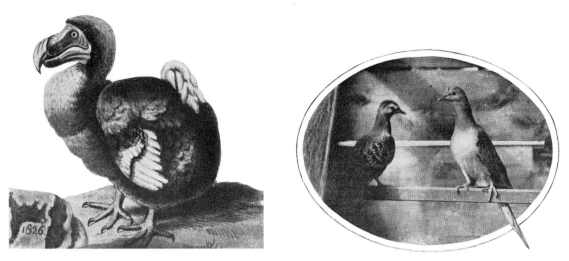

This dodo bird picture (left) was painted in 1626 and the passenger pigeons were photographed in 1898. Today both these creatures are extinct.

animal is extinct. Extinct animals are gone forever.

Since the year 1600, at least 134 birds and mammals have become extinct. The passenger pigeon is one of them. Once there were billions of passenger pigeons. People shot the pigeons for food and sport. The last passenger pigeon died in 1914. Like the dodo bird, Labrador duck, and hundreds of other animals, the passenger pigeon is gone forever.

Today's endangered animals are in trouble because of people. Some have been hunted too much. Sea turtles have been hunted for their meat, shells, and eggs. Bears, otters, wild cats, and seals have been

Above: American alligator
Right: Great egret

hunted for their fur. Whales, bison, and wild cattle have been hunted for their meat. Egrets, swans, and pelicans have been hunted for their feathers. The rhino has been killed for its horns and the elephant for its ivory tusks.

Above: African white rhino
Right: Trumpeter swan

Crocodiles and alligators have been killed for their skins.

Some endangered animals, such as leopards and wolves, will eat farm animals. The farmers kill the wild animals. Then these

Brown pelican

Hibernating Indiana bat

endangered animals become more endangered.

People use poison to kill insects. But the poison can kill bats and other animals that eat the insects.

The poison may wash into rivers and oceans. Fish swallow the poison. Brown pelicans and eagles eat the fish and become poisoned. Soon there are fewer pelicans and eagles. When very few animals of a kind are left, they are rare. Rare animals are endangered.

An animal may become rare because we poison or destroy its food. The black-footed ferret is a large weasel. It eats prairie dogs. Ranchers in the western United States have poisoned thousands of prairie dogs. The black-footed ferret has

Prairie dog

The nene is an endangered
Hawaiian goose.

become one of the
world's rarest animals.

Animals brought by man
into an area cause
problems, too. The
endangered Aleutian Canada
goose lives on islands off
Alaska. Farmers brought the

first foxes to the islands. These foxes killed nearly all the geese.

Farm animals were brought to Hawaii. Some escaped. They destroyed the forest home of wild animals. Rats and mongooses were brought to Hawaii, too. They killed wild birds. Sixty-five Hawaiian animals became extinct. Twenty-nine are endangered.

Other rare animals are in great danger because they have very few babies. The

The endangered condor lives in the mountains of southern California.

California condor is huge. But it has tiny families. The mother condor lays just one egg every two years.

Too many monkeys and parrots have been caught by pet traders. The pet traders have helped endanger these animals.

The biggest reason for so many endangered animals, however, is lack of space.

The world population keeps growing. People use more and more land for farms, homes, cities, and roads. Trees are cut. Grassland is plowed. Water is drained from wetlands. The air and water become dirty. Animals lose their homes and food.

Rabbits, robins, and squirrels can live on changed land. But most animals cannot. When they lose their homes they die.

When people change the land, they change the lives of wild animals. The Everglade kite of Florida eats apple snails. The snails live in swamps. When the swamps are drained, the snails die. The kites cannot feed themselves or their babies. The kites die.

Everglade kite

Polar bear

MEETING ENDANGERED ANIMALS

Almost every place on earth has wild animals in trouble. Endangered whales and sea turtles live in the oceans. The polar bear is in trouble in the Arctic.

Left: Orangutan
Above: Galapagos tortoise

Endangered lemurs
live on two islands
off Africa. The rare
orangutan and Philippine
monkey-eating eagle live
in Malaysia. The huge

Above: Spectacled bear
Right: Jaguar

Galapagos tortoise lives on islands off South America.

The spectacled bear is South America's only kind of bear. It has become endangered. The ocelot, margay, and jaguar are endangered, too.

Left: Giant armadillo
Above: Malayan tapir

The tapir, giant anteater, and giant armadillo are disappearing from South America. Several parrots and the Andean condor are also in trouble.

In Asia the Asiatic lion, banteng cattle, and snow leopard are endangered.

Left: Snow leopard
Above: Banteng

Fourteen kinds of pheasant have become endangered in Asian countries.

People settled in Europe a long time ago. Today most of its big animals have disappeared. The wolf, imperial eagle, brown bear, and Spanish lynx are rare.

The European bison can be seen only in a few parks.

Australia is a huge island with many unusual animals. Some of these animals carry their babies in pouches. Twenty-five pouched animals, including four kinds of kangaroos and six types of wallabies (a kangaroo cousin), are endangered. The hairy-nosed wombat and pouched wolf are in danger, too.

Kangaroos

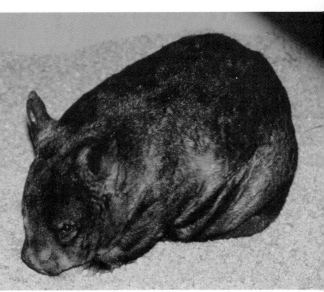

Hairy-nosed wombat

Africa has the greatest herds of four-legged animals in the world. But African people need more farmland. Many wild animals are being killed because they damage crops or are left without a home.

23

Above: Gorilla
Right: Grevy's zebra

Elephants, gorillas, rhinos, chimpanzees, and some zebras are in trouble. Also endangered are the West African ostrich, the giant eland antelope, and the gazelles of North Africa.

Bald eagle

Ostrich

North America's best-known endangered animals are the bald eagle and the whooping crane. Both birds need wild places away from people.

Grizzly bears (above), the manatee
or sea cow (below), and the Florida
panther (right) are endangered animals.

North America's big meat eaters are in trouble, too. Grizzly bears are rare. The Mexican grizzly is nearly extinct. Perhaps twenty Florida panthers are left. These big cats live in the Big Cypress Swamp and possibly in Everglades National Park.

The endangered manatee of Florida eats only water plants. Like whales, it lives in water but breathes air.

SAVING ENDANGERED ANIMALS

The list of endangered animals is becoming longer, not shorter. The list may soon include the European white stork, Dalmatian pelican, the greater prairie chicken, desert bighorn, and many more animals.

Still, some endangered animals can be saved. Endangered animals are not extinct—yet.

Desert bighorn

Greater prairie chicken

We must save these rare animals. Their kinds have been on earth for a long, long time. Many are beautiful. All of them are interesting. We can learn a great deal from these animals.

Poor countries have a hard time helping endangered animals. They cannot afford to set land aside just for animals. They cannot afford to pay people to protect the animals.

Some countries make money from endangered animals. Countries that hunt whales, for example, do not want whales protected.

Other countries do try to help endangered animals. The United States

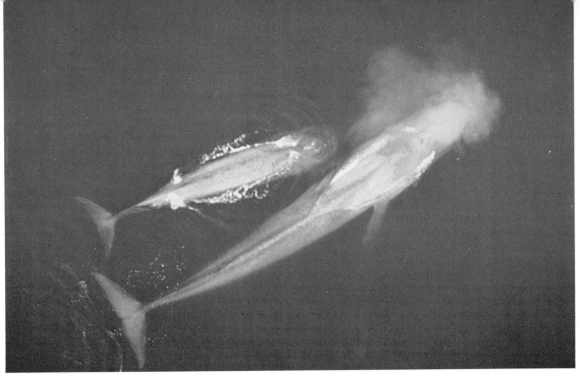

Blue whale and her baby

government passed the
Endangered Species Act in
1973. This law helps save
land just for endangered
animals. It stops people in
America from buying
endangered animals from
anywhere.

Not all countries have tough laws. A hunter in Africa may sneak into a national park. He kills a leopard. He is breaking the law, but the park is big. He is hard to catch. He knows he can sell the leopard's fur. Perhaps he cannot sell the fur in Africa, but people in another country will buy the fur for a high price.

You see, unless all countries stop selling endangered animal parts,

Grand Teton National Park (above) and
the Florida Everglades (left) provide
protection for a variety of endangered wildlife.

the animal will always be
in danger.

Saving land for
endangered animals is very
important. National parks
and wildlife refuges give
endangered animals a
chance.

With Project Tiger, India
has set aside land for some

33

of its tigers. China has saved mountain land for its giant pandas. Many African countries have huge parks for animals. North America has a number of protected parks and refuges.

Scientists help save endangered animals by learning more about them. At the Patuxent Wildlife Research Center in Maryland, scientists raise endangered animals. The International Crane

International Crane Foundation in Wisconsin studies and breeds whooping cranes.

Foundation in Wisconsin raises endangered whooping cranes.

Scientists learned that the cranes usually lay two eggs, but usually raise only one chick. Now scientists take some of the extra eggs. They raise baby cranes

35

from some of these eggs. Scientists put the other extra eggs in the nests of sandhill cranes. The wild sandhill cranes raise the whooping cranes. In 1952 only thirty-two whooping cranes were left. Now there are over one hundred in North America!

To learn more about endangered animals, scientists have many tricks. They put tiny radios on some animals. The radios send signals. Scientists can tell from the signals where the animals go.

Zoos also raise endangered animals. Animals raised in zoos may someday be released in the wild.

Zoos have some animals that are extinct in the wild. The only herds of Father David's deer in the world

Father David's deer can only be found in zoos.

Przewalski's horse

A male pronghorn antelope

exist in zoos. The last Przewalski's horses are probably the ones in zoos.

Some endangered animals can be helped. The American buffalo was almost extinct in 1900. Now there are thousands. The wood duck, trumpeter swan, pronghorn antelope,

Arabian oryx (left) and brightly
colored wood duck (above)

European ibex, and koala
have also been saved.

The Arabian oryx is nearly
extinct in Asia. But, like
many animals, it is being
raised in zoos and on wild
animal farms. Some oryx
have already been returned
to their desert home.

Young Indian lion

Bison or buffalo

Giant anteater

ENDANGERED ANIMALS NEED YOUR HELP

Endangered animals need safe, protected homes. They need to be safe from hunters and development. They need laws that will stop people from selling them. And they need your help.

Write to a government conservation office. Find out what animals are endangered near your home. Learn more about them.

Look for endangered animals when you visit a zoo. (Watch for the endangered animal sign.)

Volunteer to work at a park or refuge for endangered animals.

Don't buy wild animals as pets.

This vanishing animal symbol on the rhino pen at a zoo tells visitors that these animals are endangered.

Join a group that supports endangered animals.

Remember, when an animal becomes extinct, a type of life on our planet is lost forever.

Seals (above), margay wildcats
(right), and African elephants (below)
need to be protected from hunters.

A SELECT LIST OF 200 ENDANGERED SPECIES WORLDWIDE

For a complete list, write the U.S. Fish and Wildlife Service, Publications Unit, Washington, D.C. 20240. (The complete list includes nearly 800 animals.)

AFRICA

Mammals

Antelope, giant sable
Aye-aye
Bontebok
Cheetah
Chimpanzees
Deer, Barbary
Eland, western giant
Elephant, African
Gazelles (7 species)
Gorillas
Hyena, brown
Lemurs
Leopard
Manatee, West African
Mandrill
Monkeys (7 species)
Rhinoceros
Zebra, Grevy's
Zebra, mountain

Birds

Ostrich, West African
Rockfowl, white-necked

Reptiles

Crocodile (4 species)
Tortoise, radiated
Turtle, geometric

Amphibians

Toad, Cameroon

ARCTIC REGION

Mammals

Bear, brown
Bear, polar

ASIA

Mammals

Babirusa
Banteng
Bear, brown
Camel, Bactrian
Cat, leopard
Cat, marbled
Deer, Father David's
Deer, musk
Deer, swamp
Elephant, Asian
Gazelle, Arabian
Gazelle, sand
Gibbons
Horse, Przewalski's
Hyena, Barbary
Langur (9 species)
Leopard
Leopard, clouded
Leopard, snow
Lion, Asiatic
Macaque, lion-tailed
Orangutan
Oryx, Arabian
Rhinoceros (3 species)
Seledang (guar)
Siamang
Stag, Kashmir
Tiger
Yak, wild

Birds

Crane, black-necked
Crane, hooded
Crane, Japanese
Crane, Siberian white
Crane, white-naped
Eagle, Philippine monkey-eating
Egret, Chinese
Hornbill, helmeted
Ibis, Japanese crested
Ostrich, Arabian
Owl, giant scops
Pheasants (14 species)

Reptiles

Alligator, Chinese
Crocodile (5 species)
Gavial
Monitor (3 species)
Python, Indian

Amphibians

Salamander, Chinese giant
Salamander, Japanese giant

Fish

Ala Balik (trout)
Catfish, giant
Nekogigi (catfish)

AUSTRALIA and NEW ZEALAND

Mammals

Bandicoot (3 species)
Kangaroo, eastern gray
Kangaroo, red
Kangaroo, western gray
Rat, kangaroo (5 species)

Birds

Parakeet, hooded
Parrot, Australian
Thrush, New Zealand

Reptiles

Crocodile, saltwater
Tuatara

EUROPE

Mammals

Bear, brown
Chamois, Apennine
Ibex, Pyrenean
Lynx, Spanish

Birds

Eagle, Spanish imperial
Gull, Audouin's

HAWAIIAN ISLANDS

Birds

Coot, Hawaiian
Duck, Hawaiian
Duck, Laysan
Gallinule, Hawaiian
Goose, Hawaiian (Nene)
Honeycreeper (9 species)
Hawk, Hawaiian
Stilt, Hawaiian

NORTH AMERICA and CENTRAL AMERICA

Mammals

Bat, gray
Bat, Indiana
Bear, grizzly
Bison, wood
Bobcat, Mexican
Caribou, woodland
Cougar, eastern
Deer, Columbian white-tailed
Deer, key
Ferret, black-footed
Fox, northern swift
Jaguarundi
Manatee, West Indian
Mouse, salt marsh harvest
Otter, southern sea
Panther, Florida
Prairie dog, Mexican
Pronghorn, Sonoran
Wolf, gray (except Alaska)
Wolf, red

Birds

Condor, California
Crane, whooping
Curlew, Eskimo
Eagle, Greenland white-tailed
Eagle, bald
Falcon, peregrine
Goose, Aleutian Canada
Kite, Everglade
Parrot, Cuban
Parrot, imperial
Parrot, Puerto Rican
Pelican, brown
Prairie chicken, Attwater's greater
Quetzal, resplendent
Sparrow, dusky seaside
Warbler, Bachman's
Warbler, Kirtland's
Woodpecker, imperial
Woodpecker, ivory-billed

Reptiles

Alligator, American
Boa (4 species)
Chuckwalla, San Esteban Island
Crocodile, American
Crocodile, Cuban
Crocodile, Morelet's
Iguana (13 species)
Lizard, blunt-nosed leopard
Snake, eastern indigo
Snake, San Francisco garter
Tortoise, desert
Turtle, aquatic box

Amphibians

Salamander, Santa Cruz
Salamander, Texas blind
Toad, Houston
Treefrog, pine barrens

Fish

Chub (6 species)
Darter (8 species)
Pike, blue

Pupfish (5 species)
Sturgeon, short-nose
Trout (6 species)

Invertebrates

Snails (9 species)
Mussels (20 species)
Butterflies (10 species)

OCEANIC

Mammals

Seal, Caribbean monk
Seal, Hawaiian
Seal, Mediterranean
Whales (8 species)

Reptiles

Turtles, sea (6 species)

SOUTH AMERICA

Mammals

Armadillo, giant
Bear, spectacled
Chinchilla
Deer, marsh
Deer, pampas
Jaguar
Manatee, Amazonian
Margay (also N.A.)
Marmoset, cotton-top
Monkey (7 species)
Ocelot (also N.A.)
Otter (3 species)
Sloth, Brazilian three-toed
Tamarin (3 species)
Tapir (3 species)
Vicuna
Wolf, maned

Birds

Condor, Andean
Eagle, harpy
Grebe, Atitlan
Hawk, Galapagos
Macaw (3 species)
Parakeet, ochre-marked
Parrot, red-spectacled
Penguin, Galapagos
Rhea, Darwin's

Reptiles

Caiman (3 species)
Crocodile, Orinoco
Tortoise, Galapagos

WORDS YOU SHOULD KNOW

conservation(kahn • ser • VAY • shun) — the careful use and protection of natural resources

development(di • VEL • op • ment) — the building up of an area with new farms, homes, or businesses

endanger(en • DAIN • jer) — to put into a dangerous position

extinct(x • TINCT) — no longer living or existing

pouch(POWCH) — a part of an animal's body that is like a bag or pocket

refuge(REF • yooje) — an area where animals can live safely from danger

rare(RAIR) — not found, seen, or happening very often

tusk(TUHSK) — a long, pointed tooth that extends outside the mouth of certain animals

INDEX

About the author

Lynn M. Stone was born and raised in Meriden, Connecticut. He received his undergraduate degree from Aurora College in Illinois and his master's degree from Northern Illinois University. Once a teacher in Sarasota, Florida, Mr. Stone currently teaches English to junior high school students in the West Aurora Public School system.

A free-lance wildlife photographer and journalist, Lynn has had his work appear in many publications including National Wildlife, Ranger Rick, Oceans, Country Gentleman, Animal Kingdom, *and* International Wildlife. *He has also contributed to Time-Life, National Geographic, Audubon Field Guide, and Hallmark Cards publications.*

Many of Lynn Stone's photographs have been used in the New True Books published by Childrens Press.